...reat Britain in 2010

...photographs © Jason Friend / Jason Friend Photography Ltd.
...of all of the images in this book via: www.jasonfriend.co.uk/spiritofthehighlands

...loguing-in-Publication Data
...is title is available from the British Library

...0 016 0

...Ryelands Industrial Estate,
...ington, Somerset TA21 9PZ
...77
...96
...sgrove.com

...star Ltd, part of the Halsgrove group of companies
...l Halsgrove titles is available at: www.halsgrove.com

...d in China by Toppan Leefung Printing Ltd

GW00646711

SPIRIT O

HIGHL

JASON FR

First published in G

Copyright text and
Prints are available

All rights reserved.
stored in a retrieva
means without the

British Library Cata
A CIP record for th

ISBN 978 0 8571

PiXZ Books
Halsgrove House,
Bagley Road, Wel
Tel: 01823 6537
Fax: 01823 2167
email: sales@hal

An imprint of Hal
Information on a

Printed and boun

Introduction

The Scottish Highlands region is unquestionably the most dramatic mountain scenery to be found within the British Isles. Characteristic views of lochs, ancient woodlands and mountains abound and whilst the famous locations such as Rannoch Moor, Loch Ness and Eilean Donan Castle are obvious tourist hotspots, the lesser known glens and lochs are equally memorable.

Covering approximately half of the Scottish mainland, the Highlands stretch from the shores of Loch Lomond to Sutherland in the far north. The highest British peak, Ben Nevis, stands aloft the Great Glen, which runs from Loch Linnhe on the west coast to the Highland capital city of Inverness on the east. Near here, the Cairngorm National Park is home to the second and third highest peaks and can lay claim to being the largest area of upland sub-arctic wilderness within the United Kingdom.

However it is not just the natural features of the Highlands that dominate the vista. Past and present human occupiers have left their mark on the landscape with numerous castles, villages and towns situated in some of the most remarkable of natural locations. Although human intervention has not just been limited to constructing dwellings and forts, with vast tracts of the once great Caledonian Forest being destroyed by mankind, it could be argued that it is the combination of natural features and human influence that has helped to create the unquestionably Scottish landscape that we all now know and love so much.

Within this book I hope to share with you not only some of my favourite locations within the Highlands, but also some of the majestic natural scenes that I have been lucky enough to witness through my quest to capture the spirit of the Highlands.

Acknowledgements

Thank you once more to Steven Pugsley and the rest of the team at Halsgrove for making this book a reality.

I would like to whole-heartedly thank all of my family and friends who constantly offer support and encouragement including John Friend, Penny, Roy and Mark Whitehouse and Valerie Hodgkins.

Thank you to my wife Lynette who has been there to support and encourage me whenever I have needed it most, and my baby boy Rhys who joined me on a trip to the Highlands at the tender age of four months – and will hopefully accompany me on many more to come.

Opposite page:
Cloud formations illuminated by the setting sun,
reflected in Loch Lochy.

Castle Stalker near Port Appin is a four-storey Tower House located on a tidal islet on Loch Laich, an inlet off Loch Linnhe.

Opposite page:
Eilean Donan Castle reflected in the still waters of Loch Duich at dusk.

Looking towards Glen Carron from the banks of Loch Carron,
a sea loch shown here at low tide.

Opposite page:
Traffic at dusk on the dramatic Pass of Glencoe.

A wild primrose (Primula Vulgaris) growing wild in the Highlands.

Red Deer stag in a small patch of Highland woodland.

Left:
Evening light illuminates the red hues of the wild mountain landscape of Glen Sligachan on the Isle of Skye. Although an island, Skye is now connected to the mainland by a controversial road bridge.

Slioch, a mountain alongside Loch Maree in the Beinn Eighe National Nature Reserve which was Britain's first National Nature Reserve.

Sailing boats moored near the busy port of Ullapool on the shores of Loch Broom.

Opposite page:
Dramatic clouds and Cairngorm mountains reflected upon Loch Morlich.

Late afternoon light illuminates the woodland fringing Loch Etive in the Argyll and Bute region.

Opposite page:
A picturesque view of Loch Leven and surrounding mountains.

Frost-covered ferns, photographed in the Rothiemurchus Estate.

Late afternoon sun on the face of Carn Dearg in the snow-covered Glen Nevis.

The ruins of Strome Castle, situated
alongside Loch Carron.

Opposite page:
Woodland near the Falls of Foyers,
upon the banks of Loch Ness
located in Glen Albyn.

Left:
Sailing boats moored on Loch Leven near Ballachulish, looking towards Beinn Bhan, Sgorr Bhan and Sgorr Dhearg.

Rain clears revealing the mountain peaks surrounding Little Loch Broom.

Left:
Looking towards the
Coigach Mountain range
from moorland above
Loch Lurgainn.

A stretch of the West Highland Way, a popular long distance hiking route, between Fort William and Kinlochleven.

A storm clears behind the peaks
surrounding Loch Laggan.

Opposite page:
The River Garry and surrounding
woodland, near the Pass of
Killiecrankie.

Single track mountain road heading down
Glen Gloy near the Great Glen.

Opposite page:
Clearing storm clouds above
Loch Assynt near Lochinver.

The fast-flowing falls of the River Pattack and surrounding woodland.

Opposite page:
The autumnal colours of oak woodlands fringing Loch Lomond at the bay of Milarrochy.

Loch Garten fringed by the Abernethy Forest.

Right:
Arklet Falls and Sniad Burn
near Inversnaid
during autumn.

33

Looking across the rocky shoreline north of Elgol on the Isle of Skye,
towards the peaks of the Black Cuillins.

Rua Reidh Lighthouse, located along the coast near Gairloch.

Opposite page:
Pocket of Scots pine amidst the open landscape of the Dirrie More near Braemore.

Woodland reflected in the still waters of Loch Milton near Boat of Garten.

A single tree on the barren landscape of the Pass of Glen Coe.

Opposite page: Rainbow over the banks of Loch Lomond and nearby mountains in the Loch Lomond and the Trossachs National Park.

Young trees planted as part of the Bad na Sgalag native
pinewood regeneration project near Gairloch.

A sequence of canal locks on the Caledonian Canal near Fort Augustus.

Left:
A cascade of peat-coloured water at
Rogie Falls, near Contin.

The dominating mountain landscape of Glen Coe.

Opposite page:
Scots pines in the Beinn Eighe National Nature Reserve, remnants of the great Caledonian Forest which once covered the Scottish Highlands from coast to coast.

Moss-covered tree upstream of the Eas Chia-aig waterfall.

Opposite page:
Stac Pollaidh (also known as "Stack Polly") is an impressive mountain found in the Assynt area, located north of Ullapool. Despite its dramatic appearance, it is only 613 metres (2009 feet) in height.

The frozen Lower Falls located in Glen Nevis under the shadow of Ben Nevis.

Storm clouds gather over Loch Tummel viewed from the viewpoint know as Queen's View.

The Corran ferry port with hoarfrost-covered woodland behind.

Left:
Urquhart Castle on the banks of
Loch Ness, Great Glen.

The pinks and reds of a west-coast sunset viewed from Oban,
looking towards the Western Isles.

Frost -covered shoreline of
a bay on Loch Linnhe,
viewed at dusk.

The Commando Memorial near Spean Bridge in the Great Glen commemorates the commandos who trained in the area during the Second World War.

Highland cattle stand resistant to the harsh winter environment of Glen Dochart.

Opposite page:
Cloud formations reflected upon Loch Garry.

Left:
Countryside surrounding the village of
Gairloch on the banks of Loch Gairloch.

The Isle of Skye viewed across Loch Gairloch from the Wester Ross village of Gairloch.

Clouds at sunset reflected upon the still waters of the River Calder running through Glen Banchor near Newtonmore and the Monadhliath Mountains.

Opposite page:
Clouds clear from the peak of Cùl Beag, a mountain in the Assynt parish of Sutherland.

The subtle shades of a mid-winter's day reflected in Loch a' Chuilinn, near Lochluichart.

Clearing storm reveals the features of the mountains of Strathconon.

A rainbow over Loch Ness,
Great Glen.

Opposite page:
The dramatic ruins of Ardvreck Castle
located on a rocky promontory that
juts into Loch Assynt. The castle was
constructed by the MacLeods of
Assynt during two phases in
1500 and 1590.

Lochan an Stainge located on Rannoch Moor with the dominating peak of the
Black Mount and surrounding mountains in the distance.